Rainer Krumm
Christian Buchholz

30 Minutes

Innovation Culture

Bibliographic information from the German National Library
The German National Library lists this publication in the German National Bibliography. Detailed bibliographic information can be found online at http://dnb.d-nb.de.

ISBN 978-3-86936-842-9

Cover design: die imprimatur, Hainburg
Cover concept: Martin Zech Design, Bremen
Editing: Happenstance Type-O-Rama, Oakland, USA
Graphics: 9 Levels Institute for Value Systems GmbH & Co KG
Author photos: Petra Rückert
Set: Zerosoft, Timisoara (Romania)
Printing and processing: Print-on-demand

First published under the title "30 Minuten Innovationskultur" in 2020 by GABAL Verlag, Germany

www.9levels.com

You'll know more in 30 minutes!

This book is designed to enable you to absorb concise and sound information in a short time. With the help of a guidance system, you will be led through the book. This will allow you to grasp the essentials within your personal time allotment (from 10 to 30 minutes).

Short reading time

You can read the whole book in 30 minutes. If you have less time, read only those passages that contain important information.

- **All important information is printed in grey.**

- Key questions with page references at the beginning of each chapter allow for quick orientation: you turn directly to the page that closes your knowledge gap.

- *Numerous summaries within the chapters allow for skimming.*

- The "Fast Reader" at the end of the book summarizes all important information.

- An index makes it easier to find what you are looking for.

Contents

Preface

Innovation is today not only a factor in a company's image but simply vital for survival. Being innovative is also a must if companies want to to be in the lead tomorrow.

Much is being done to promote innovation. Creativity techniques, innovation processes, design thinking, and innovation labs—the list of approaches is long, and new ones are added regularly. But often what works well in other companies remains completely ineffective in one's own organization or leads to sometimes very strong resistance in implementation.

In such cases, something crucial was often overlooked: innovation initiatives must take into account the existing corporate culture. Not everything that is possible makes sense. Rather, only the steps and methods appropriate to the respective company are the true success drivers. This guide, *30 Minutes on Innovation Culture,* will clearly demonstrate that innovation is feasible for every company—if you consider the corporate culture. In this book, individual corporate cultures are broken down with the help of the so-called 9 Levels of Value Systems, a model for differentiating between value systems. You can better understand your own company, can get to know helpful tools, are introduced to concrete ideas on how to create a culture of innovation in your company, and can learn which techniques fit your corporate culture. Practical examples ensure

that the possibilities for implementation in everyday corporate life become tangible.
We wish you every success in establishing a culture of innovation in your company.

Rainer Krumm & Christian Buchholz

Become an innovation culture ninja!

This book is designed to give you an overview of the topic of innovation culture in 30 minutes.
But of course there is so much more to learn about it.
The authors have prepared a website that provides even more inspiration and knowledge, as well as practical tools for developing a culture of innovation in your organization:
www.innovationculture.ninja
See you there!

30 MINUTES

1. Innovation culture

"How do I manage to **be innovative with my company?**" This is a question that those at companies of all sizes ask themselves, because today only those who stand out from the crowd with a service or product will be able to survive in the market in the long term.

Many methods and approaches support the companies willing to change, but often the development of an innovation culture gets stuck and **does not make progress**. The reason often lies in the selection of the wrong instruments or the wrong application of these methods.

A better understanding of the **mechanisms of value orientation and innovation culture** helps companies to take the right steps and drive the change process forward.

1.1 Conditions for a culture of innovation

Reducing costs and improving products are usually the first measures that companies take to remain competitive. Although it has long since ceased to be an insider tip that innovation culture is also an important success factor, companies are often overburdened with the task of selecting the right instruments, leadership principles, and management systems for a high-performance innovation culture. Companies often look for a **patent remedy**. Some have launched initiatives such as research and development activities or innovation departments, or even created their own incubators for start-ups. All this should have produced good results, one would think. But for many, the output is still unsatisfactory.

Examples of radical changes

Those who not only develop their business model and product portfolio but are also able to radically change it if the market makes it possible are successful in the long term. Here are some examples:

Google

Google is not only established in web applications but has now also extended its reach in the direction of the automotive industry with self-driving cars (Waymo), the production of fiber optic networks (Fiber), and biotechnology and genetic engineering (Calico).

Ford

With its new business unit Ford Smart Mobility headquartered in Silicon Valley, the car manufacturer Ford has set up a business unit that deals with models for car sharing and the development of apps for finding parking spaces.

Lego

With its new business model, the toy manufacturer Lego is involving its customers in the development of new products and in the innovation processes of design and market research. In the meantime, kits created by customers have become bestsellers.

Many companies, especially in medium-sized businesses, see innovation from the perspective of their existing products. They focus on making an existing product even better. Companies that supply the retail trade, for example, view the retailer as a customer and overlook the end consumer and his needs. For this reason, it is not enough to offer an additional sales channel simply by setting up an online shop, for example. Something unprecedented is needed. Old ideas must be scrapped and partially replaced by completely new (digital) business models.

Flat hierarchies

Researchers in the field of Motivation agree that employees are much more satisfied if they can act in a self-determined manner. But those who are literally trapped in a hierarchy usually do not have much freedom of choice. The consequences of this are also generally known, as they are reflected in high sickness rates and internal dismissal. These are all terms that have been on the minds of the media, but also of managers, for years.

However, flat hierarchies do not only produce happier employees; in addition to a lower sickness rate, companies also benefit from the fact that their employees are more innovative.

A current study by the management consultancy company Kienbaum in cooperation with job placement agency StepStone shows that 61 percent of **companies with fewer hierarchical levels are more innovative**, and in particular their employees produce significantly more ideas. Of the employees of strongly hierarchically structured companies, only a third perceive their employer as innovative. If employees have the freedom to organize themselves, they not only are more satisfied but also feel more closely connected to the company. They become more self-motivated and less slowed down and are therefore more likely to give free rein to their creativity and develop new things. This freedom has two positive side effects that have a direct impact on the **profitability of companies**:

1. Greater employee satisfaction automatically reduces the cost of staff absences due to illness.
2. Companies whose employees are satisfied are more innovative.

In this context, we can further substantiate the statement made above: "Innovation is often misunderstood in medium-sized businesses," Stephan Wegerer, former head of Innovation Management at the Adidas Group, told *WirtschaftsWoche Online*. Although companies are well aware that the end consumer is the actual customer, on whom it is better to focus, unfortunately this insight is still not being put into practice.

A total of 14,000 specialists and managers were interviewed in the mentioned Kienbaum study. Of the specialists surveyed, 74 percent stated that they work in a company with a strongly developed hierarchy, and 18 percent had the impression that the management level did not desire employees to contribute ideas and suggestions for improvement. And 68 percent of the managers were of the opinion that they work in a company with a strong hierarchy. According to Kienbaum's managing director, Walter Jochmann, **the German economy for example is still giving away far too much innovation potential**. If hierarchies were abolished, responsibility delegated, and employees involved in management decisions, companies would be economically more successful.

Supportive leaders

However, not only the hierarchy inhibits the establishment of a culture of innovation. Another reason is leadership. Depending on the **management system**, employees are more satisfied, more motivated, and corre-

spondingly more innovative. If managers grant their employees a higher degree of **self-determination** and thus more **personal responsibility**, this in turn leads to these employees identifying more with the company and being more committed to becoming innovative.
However, because such a management style has not yet reached all management levels, the bosses often do not appear in a very good light from the point of view of the employees: a full two-thirds believe that their superiors are not well prepared for the challenges that the future will bring.
In complete contrast to this view is the self-assessment of managers with regard to their own performance. They are convinced that, on the one hand, they have their management job well under control with regard to their vision of the future and that, on the other hand, they are seen by their employees as a role model for success and performance. This **gap between the self-image of managers and the external image** from the perspective of their employees shows that experience and reality are far apart on this issue. So there are still enough starting points for personnel and organizational developers.
Not only top management is in demand when it comes to innovation culture. Above all, the **second and third management levels** have a decisive influence on how the innovation potential of employees is used.

Resources

Whether a company is really prepared to support creative projects can be seen from the resources it makes available for this. It's easy to have good ideas, but when resources in the form of money, people, or tools are needed, you can see **whether a company is really serious about innovation** or not.

If resources are used for innovative projects, they are lacking elsewhere. **Employees** who can no longer carry out their actual activities, as well as funds for **budgets** that are now no longer available for previously planned areas, are the price that must be paid for a stronger focus on innovation.

Another obstacle to innovation is the focus on quick success.. Most of the measures in the operational area show effects quite quickly. Innovations, on the other hand, are frequently not measurable in the short term and can often only be assessed in terms of their success in the medium term. Disruptive ideas in particular often fail because they **simply cannot be measured with classic managing tools.**

For this reason, it is perhaps understandable that some companies are reluctant to allocate many resources for innovative projects.

Most companies provide resources but are **not consistent in their actions**. Whenever the importance of innovation is weighed against the urgency of day-to-day operations, the daily business usually wins.

Time as a resource plays a special role in this context: it is a major point of discussion in companies that want to establish innovation. Due to the daily to-dos, the majority feels unable to find time to develop ideas. Allowing free space is therefore an essential prerequisite for a functioning innovation culture.

Teams and their composition

Where do innovations come from? Where do they originate? Exactly—in people's minds. Behind every innovation is ingenuity, passion, and certainly also a portion of courage. No machine, no artificial intelligence can emulate this.. Especially a diverse team , In particular, a diverse team, **with people of different professions, gender, cultural backgrounds** can be incredibly enriching for an innovation process.

In an organisational world, everything revolves around roles and functions. This makes people interchangeable. It is quite different in the development of innovation. Here, the individuals are more important than the function. *If, for example, two warehouse specialists pick the goods for a customer, the container will definitely contain what is marked on the shipping documents. It makes no difference whether the order picker is a gifted recreational footballer, a drummer in a rock group, or a Greenpeace supporter in Antarctica every winter. In the overall system of warehouse management, it does not matter. But when it comes to creativity and innovation, the situation looks completely different.*

Anyone who wants to put together and lead innovation teams must pay **attention to diversity**. In addition to different ethnicities and genders, this also means different age groups, CVs, skills, and personalities. Developing these individuals into an effective team is an essential task of leadership.

Incentive systems

The design of a company's incentive systems has a great influence on the innovative output of an organization. Only **about one in four companies** generally measures employees by how often they contribute ideas and how often this ideas turn into innovations. Employees tend to push the activities that influence the assessment of their skills. In most companies, **day-to-day business** has **a much higher priority than developing ideas**. In general, employees have no intention to hide their ideas, but they align their actions with the desired goals. If the submission of ideas, the courage to think in new ways, and the implementation of **innovations is rewarded**, this dramatically increases the probability that employees will continue to be active in the area of innovation in the future.

Do you reward innovation?

Review the incentive systems in your company:

- Is there a chance of promotion for employees who bring in a lot of good ideas?
- Are your managers sensitized to the topics of creativity and innovation?

- Are employees measured by the number and quality of their ideas?
- Are you tolerant of bad ideas?
- How free are your employees to be allowed to circumvent existing rules?

Communication

If you come to a highly innovative company as an external person, you will quickly notice that **communication is different**. Although there are departments and structures, the doors are open in the figurative sense even when there is physical separation. Everywhere you meet people who stand together and **collaborate** on new **projects** . If you need different knowledge and connections of a kind that does not exist within the company, **networks** are called in. For new projects, those employees with the ability to bring them to great success as quickly as possible are brought together.

Swarm organizations are typical for such companies. They are characterized by an extremely flat hierarchy which allows decisions to be made very quickly.

In most companies, however, the reality today still looks different: you encounter strongly hierarchical structures, separate departments, and correspondingly long and difficult decision-making processes. Networks do not exist, and if they do, they serve only the day-to-day business, not the development of ideas.

Changing the communication structures is the cheapest and fastest way to increase the innovative ability of a company. Not even the usual structures need to be changed. For example, the introduction of an **informal network** through which employees can exchange information is one way to quickly implement a change in communication. Digital technologies such as a kind of an internal social media platform can be an important part of a change. Unfortunately, much of management is rather suspicious of informal structures. The often-heard opinion is that structures, compliance with rules, and control are much easier to manage. In contrast, informal communication channels are difficult to control, monitor, and measure. Consequently, they are often argued against. The management culture must therefore change so much that, for example,

- the loss of control is seen not as a problem but as an opportunity,
- departmental or divisional boundaries can also be overcome, and
- even something not measurable has a value.

Overview: Requirements for a culture of innovation
The prerequisites for a culture of innovation are as follows:

- flat hierarchies
- supportive executives
- enough resources

- diversity in the composition of teams
- incentive systems that reward innovative ideas
- informal communication channels

30 *Those who not only develop their business model and product portfolio but radically change it are successful in the long term. If corporate hierarchies were abolished, responsibility delegated, and employees involved in management decisions, companies would be economically more successful.*

1.2 What is innovation?

A common definition of innovation is that an innovation is something new, like ideas for or inventions of products, services, or application and production processes, that is the result of a thought process. While innovation used to be the exception rather than the rule, global competition and the increasing speed of markets make it absolutely necessary for companies to be innovative today.

A look back shows that there have always been relapses in innovation throughout history. Often they were the result of total destruction by wars, years of failed harvests, or strong fluctuations in temperature and precipitation. They were **born out of necessity** and have always led to people changing also their living conditions. Today, innovation is essential for the survival of companies in particular. Those who are not innovative lag behind the competition until they have to leave the market. But it is not enough to implement an innovative project as a one-off. A company that wants to establish innovation needs a culture that permanently supports this process. It needs a culture of innovation, which makes for lasting success.

What makes innovation successful?

Is a great idea automatically an innovation? When do ideas translate to success? Is it when processes are sophisticated and thus regulate responsibilities and procedures? Does it take courageous pioneers to break rules and move projects forward even in the face of the greatest resistance? Or is it innovative when managers see a market of the future where market researchers currently believe that a market does not exist at all? Or perhaps it is the employees who generate new ideas because their environment allows them to do so, and who also have no problems implementing the ideas? But companies that pursue their visions without effort could also be innovative. All these points can be an indication of a functioning innovation culture, but they also make it clear: **there is not the right innovation culture** for every company. Highly innovative companies demonstrate this through their **individuality**. Companies invest a lot in establishing a culture of innovation. Nevertheless, many of them are dissatisfied with the results. What is it that repeatedly leads to innovation being stopped? The question must be asked differently: What is it that drives innovation?

What drives innovation?

To make a long story short, **innovation culture must be actively lived, in the way that is working for the respective company.**

We often observe a creative culture in innovative companies that works according to the **motto "fun and focus."** The organization is open to activities and focused on the implementation of ideas.

The entire creative potential available in the company is exploited here, which requires a high level of commitment from people but also investment in employees and jobs. This enables the company to react quickly to market needs and to develop and shape markets proactively.

The corporate culture is therefore important for the innovative ability of companies. This poses a further challenge for the management of innovation: if top management tries to think in new directions and is then confronted with a rather passive corporate culture, this must be included in the planning and implementation of innovation projects. Otherwise, conflicts are inevitable. It is therefore the task of top management to develop innovation measures **in line with the cultural background of the company** in order to achieve the strategic goals.

A common definition of innovation is that an innovation is something new, like ideas for or inventions of products, services, or application and production processes, that are the result of a thought process. Today, innovation is essential for the survival of companies in particular. Innovative companies have a creative culture, which can be described by the motto "fun and focus."

1.3 The current situation in companies

A Capgemini study on innovation in organizations conducted worldwide in March and April 2017, in which 1700 employees from 340 companies were surveyed came to the conclusion that **innovation capability is still not a reality in companies today**. In times of increasing digitalization, this is a major competitive disadvantage. In this context, corporate culture is seen as one of the biggest obstacles on the way to a digital organization. This view is shared by 62 percent of international and even 72 percent of German companies. In plain language, this means that **companies risk falling behind their competitors in the current digitalization environment**. The same survey was conducted in 2011, where the results were even better by 7 percentage points. Of the 340 companies surveyed, only 7 percent believe that they can quickly test and implement new ideas. The evaluators of the study clearly state that companies are obviously not able to involve their employees in cultural development. However, this is exactly what is essential for innovation culture and digital transformation.

All this shows that companies **still have a lot of work** ahead of them if they want to become an innovative organization that can be a decisive step ahead of its competitors.

A large proportion of companies today are far from being innovative. In particular, the corporate culture is considered by many as an obstacle on the way to a digital organization. The participation of the employees is crucial for the development of an innovation culture.

1.4 There is no patent remedy

One thing we can anticipate from reading this chapter: **there is no patent remedy for innovation success.** If you follow this book to the end, you will see innovation culture from a different perspective - and you will start your next innovation project with a new understanding.

But before we go into detail, it is important to understand why an approach that has worked wonderfully for one company is unlikely to produce the desired re-

sults for you. The solution to the puzzle lies in the **individuality of your company** and the people in it. You will not be able to copy the innovation culture of another successful company. The approach and the procedure must be adapted to your company and to your employees. Just as you search for and find the right people, you must also find the right innovation recipe so that it can develop its full potential. For this reason, we would like to take a small detour into the world of the **9 Levels of Value Systems**, because you need the knowledge of the value systems of people, teams, and organizations to find the right approach for establishing a culture of innovation in your company.
In the next chapter, we will examine the findings of the model of the 9 Levels of Value Systems with regard to a high-performance innovation culture.

The origin of the 9 levels

The model of the 9 levels is based on the findings and research work of Clare W. Graves (1914–1986). The professor of psychology, who was not only active in research but also worked for many years as a consultant in business enterprises, clinics, and educational institutions, placed a focus of his research on the **investigation of developmental stages of the human being**. He himself called the result of his work "an upwardly striving cyclical double helix of the development of the adult human being in his biopsychosocial system." This model was not only very complex but also

described the diversity of human development in a very multiperspective way. The so-called *Graves value system* thus represents a value model that depicts how individuals or entire systems—such as departments, companies, or organizations—think and act.
Rainer Krumm has simplified this model for application and combined a theoretical scientific model with a valid scientific analysis tool—the **9-level analysis tool**. The 9 levels and the theory of value systems represent the dynamics responsible for the development of the participants. The value systems express ways of thinking, beliefs, inner states of mind, and principles.
Every person, every group, and every organization is on a stage of development, and the different stages wind their way up like a spiral staircase. Development takes place only from level to level; a "shortcut" is not possible. We would like to describe the individual levels and thus developmental stages briefly below to prepare you for the second chapter, which is oriented toward these levels.

Why only seven levels?
We will deal only with the levels that are relevant to the topic. For this reason the first level, beige, and the last level, coral, are not used here.
The first stage of development—beige—is all about satisfying basic needs, so there is no room for innovation. The ninth level—coral—has so far only been rudimentarily described. It is emerging, but there are not many individuals, let alone groups, in coral. In any

case, it is about ego relationship, by no means only about power and prestige. Rather, it is about having an ego relatedness, which is connected with high respect for all living beings. In the economy this level plays a subordinate role. Like beige, coral is not a subject of the developed tool and is not measured.

Level purple: The community member

People on the purple level are part of a community that has a patriarch or matriarch as its leader. The leader's word is law. Rules are not questioned; obedience is a matter of course. The community itself offers protection, security, and belonging to each individual. Traditions and customs are maintained. Classic examples of purple companies are family businesses with few functional structures.

Values on the purple level

Tradition, customs, rituals, home, obedience, security, hospitality, securing of existence, passing on of traditions

Level red: The power obsessed

People on the red level see themselves as conquerors of new territories and markets. They have a strong desire for power, independence, and prestige. They are powerful and innovative and take the initiative quickly but direct everything to their own advantage. Resources can also fall victim to this. In accordance with their credo "the strongest prevails," they sometimes break rules and laws.

Values on the red level

Assertiveness, self-confidence, demanding respect, bravery, impulsiveness, aggression, egocentric thinking, courage, personal success

Level blue: The lover of order

People on the blue level seek and need rules and laws to feel comfortable. They see themselves as part of a system that can only function if guidelines and responsibilities are clearly assigned. They are extremely dutiful and disciplined, emphasize hierarchies, and attach great importance to a clear distribution of tasks and responsibilities. From their point of view, it goes without saying that others also accept these rules and live by them.

Values on the blue level

Loyalty, order, control, reliability, justice, observance of hierarchies, quality, discipline, truth, patience, observance of rules

Level orange: The goal oriented

People on the orange level, like those on level red, focus on their own success, but at the same time they look at the well-being of others and have an eye for the whole. Their goal is to achieve and maintain prosperity and to be able to show it. Further development is important to them. Those who work with them can rely on target agreements.

Values on the orange level

Productivity, competition, independence, value creation, concentration, focus on results, personal and overall success, process orientation, monetary and economic growth

Level green: The team player

People on the green level see in every achieved goal the result of the collective work. It is their ambition that the community be successful in the long run. Problems are discussed together and possible solutions are compared and weighed. Meetings, people, and relationships are more important to them than the matter at hand.

Values on the green level

Harmony, fairness, cosmopolitanism, integration of people, adaptation, responsibility for others, tolerance, consensus, dialogue, personal and human growth

Level yellow: The multiperspective thinker

People on the yellow level are the first to be able to recognize, use, and combine the strengths of the levels before them. They focus on knowledge enhancement, flexibility, competence, and independence. To possess something is secondary for them; instead they strive for competence and knowledge. To achieve this, they always select the people who can best support them in this respect.

Values on the yellow level
Self-reflection, systemic integration, creativity, knowledge, autonomy, networking, profound competence, lively growth, openness

Level turquoise: The well-being oriented

People on the turquoise level focus exclusively on the well-being of the world and direct their life and work solely toward it. They think holistically-globally, ecologically, and intuitively. They take entrepreneurial responsibility for the community and orient themselves toward nature. They see their thoughts and actions as bearing a responsibility for the future of life.

Values on the turquoise level
Sustainability, holon, acceptance of global complexity, spiritual awareness, high ideals, farsightedness, network intelligence, collective intuition, improvement of the living conditions of all forms of life

30 ***When you deal with the topic of innovation culture, you first of all face a great challenge: Innovation is still not a reality in companies. Companies risk falling behind their competitors in the current digitalization environment.***

There is no patent recipe for how a company can establish a culture of innovation.
The solution to the riddle lies in the individuality of your company and the people in it. You will never be able to copy the innovation culture of another company. The approach and the procedure must fit your organization.
Therefore, you need the knowledge of the value systems of people, teams, and organizations to find the right approach if you want to establish a culture of innovation in your company.

30 MINUTES

2. Stages of innovation culture

Every person is at his or her own personal level of development, from which point they approach the topic of innovation very individually. For example, while it is quite natural for a person at one level to see innovation as a joint project, such an approach would be completely unthinkable for someone at another level. Without this knowledge of the differences in dealing with innovation, a planned innovation project can be doomed to failure from the outset.

In this chapter we would like to introduce you to the individual levels and the typical way of dealing with innovation topics at these development stages. You will learn how the necessary interest in innovation can be stimulated at each level, which approaches work best, and which tactics can be used to make innovations goal oriented and produce results.

2.1 Purple: Innovation sovereignty of the owner

Normally there are 9 levels in this system. However, since the first level, beige, is all about survival—that is, ensuring basic needs, such as food intake, protection, and reproduction—there is no time for innovation at this stage of development. From an entrepreneurial point of view, this means that a self-employed person who is currently fighting for his or her economic survival will hardly have time to think about innovation processes. Rather, new ideas are born, if at all, by chance.

At the purple level, the next stage, there are certainly innovative products and processes, but innovation culture at this stage of development is not an essential part of the strategy. Everything revolves around the corporate leader, who as patriarch or matriarch holds the reins on the one hand and is often the one who is him- or herself considered a tinkerer and inventor on the other. So practically everything that has to do with innovation and development crosses his or her desk.

Examples

A **mechanical engineer** *from Swabia, owner of the company and himself an engineer, started many years ago with a disruptive idea in the market and was successful. In the eyes of his employees, he is a shining light with innovation sovereignty; everyone is looking at him.*

He is the one who invents new things, and ideas from other employees often find no place next to him. Sometimes he withdraws from the actual business of managing the company in order to develop something new again.
At the German confectionery manufacturer HARIBO, the company owner Hans Riegel Jr. was the creative inventor of many innovative products and developed jelly beans and other sweets in his small studio and laboratory.

Dangers

The notion of the lonely inventor who locks him- or herself in his or her workshop and comes out with great ideas has long been outdated. **Innovations that are successful on the market are always the result of the interplay of many different skills. Diversity is a decisive factor for lasting innovation success.** Of course, employees have good ideas even in a purple culture, but to push them forward they to be very smart. It is not uncommon for an inventive employee to present his or her idea as if it were the idea of the company owner. Then their chances of being heard are probably better.
Whether this leads to a motivating culture of ideas is more than questionable. Frustrations are therefore common for employees in a purple company. The consequence is that **creative minds leave the company quickly** because they do not want to keep on fighting against management policy.

Tips

In our view, innovative ideas of the team can only be successful at the purple level if the **owner is involved at an early stage**. If he or she is involved from the beginning and is part of the process, things can turn out quite differently.

For the establishment of an innovation culture at the purple level the help of a neutral third party as moderator is useful. Otherwise the patriarch or matriarch will quickly fall back into his or her usual pattern of behavior.

30 *Disruptive innovations often have a tough time with purple if they were not developed by the company founder him- or herself. However, a culture of innovation can be established at this stage of development if the owner is involved in early ideation workshops, for example.*

2.2 Red: Success-driven idea development

At the red level, ideas are primarily used to consolidate one's own position. The pronounced EGO-reference on the red level leads to people being reluctant to share ideas until they are ready for discussion. This behavior can be increased if the individual receives high incentives for submitted ideas. This creates a culture in which people keep ideas to themselves for fear that someone else might use them and take advantage of them. Structured idea development with many participants is often seen as a waste of time, and the focus is on rapid success with new ideas. New ideas, whose implementation makes the individual employee more successful, are often implemented very quickly and, if necessary, even against existing rules.

Examples

A young start-up from the **fintech sector** *enters the market with a disruptive idea aimed at radically changing the established banking market. All employees are working with high energy on this project, and sometimes all free time is subordinated to this goal. The main driver for action is the prospect of high financial returns, because employees participate in the company's success with company shares and are eager to bring the company to the stock market after the product launch.*

In a **telemarketing company**, *so-called innovation battles are held. Small teams compete against each other in a kind of contest for the better ideas. The sales manager is the one-person jury. The winners are determined in a knock-out round and are rewarded with cash payouts to the small teams. The respective winners then move on to the next battle. In the final round, the winning team is dissolved and its members may compete against each other. The winner is the innovation champion and receives an incentive luxury trip for two people.*

Dangers

Innovation processes must achieve **quickly verifiable results** for companies at the red level. In contrast to companies at the purple level, **sustainability** is of **secondary importance**. The focus is always on the question, What is in it for us? Quick successes are more attractive than long-term changes.

Tips

Red organizations love competition. **Innovations often arise from direct competition** and rivalry. The important thing here is that the winner must stand out as someone special. The pressure that arises because you don't want to lose is definitely desirable. **Direct reward systems** work wonders here in the innovation process. In addition, momentum and dynamics in the innovation process are important for red.

30 *Structured idea development is not desired at the red level; ideas must instead bring rapid success. Incentives significantly increase the commitment to idea generation.*

2.3 Blue: Ideas flow through systems

Blue works in a very structured and process-oriented way. This procedure is of course also followed in innovation projects. Since creative approaches do not fit into blue thinking patterns, an attempt is made to tame them with new processes and rules. This is why blue companies often have an elaborate company suggestion system or even a separate department for innovation management. Every idea that is born thus flows into a process and is evaluated according to previously defined criteria.

Examples

German car manufacturers *have had a good position in the market for many years because they can ensure consistently high quality through continuous development. The focus here is on the further development of existing products; disruptive technologies such as electromobility are only hesitantly anticipated. The industry is not a pioneer here.*

A **very innovative pharmaceutical company** *has reorganized its innovation process after a period of rapid growth. For this purpose, an innovation department was established, which developed a multilevel innovation portal that works as follows: Anyone who has an idea can contribute it. A steering committee then decides whether the idea is relevant and sustainable, whereupon the gates are opened for the next stage, where further resources are subsequently made available. In this way, the innovation process is very structured and organized. In order to get more innovations into the process, methods that are actually common at the orange level, such as incentives, are* *now being established. But there is also a blue-level problem to be solved, which may sound banal at first glance, but is nevertheless important: To which working time account can the innovation hours be billed?*

Dangers

New ideas must go through a rather **lengthy process** at blue. Sometimes it takes several months or even years for an idea to pass through the various decision-making stages—often a frustrating experience for the person who submitted the idea. In addition, the idea is diluted more and more as it passes through several levels of the hierarchy and often has little to do with the original idea in the end. This is the reason why many creative minds leave blue cultures or at some point stop thinking about alternative paths. The widespread **desire to avoid mistakes** at this stage of development also means that risky ideas often don't stand a chance. Disruptive innovations are not to be expected in blue cultures.

Tips

Blue organizations are often very strong in **incremental innovation**—the structured development of existing products and services. Brainstorming in blue organizations works very well with **process-oriented brainstorming workshops**. Facilitators who like to work with abstract creative methods will not get ahead or will encounter resistance in blue teams. Brainstorming with blue teams in innovation workshops can work quite well outside the organizational processes. It is important that people from different hierarchical and organizational levels come together here. This increases both the quality of the ideas as well as the probability of implementation. The way the ideas gained are handled after the event is also important. In order to prevent frustration, the suggestions should be processed transparently and the idea providers should ideally be involved in the implementation.

If a blue culture has to adapt very quickly and adopt new approaches due to changes in the market, it may make sense to set up a **second organization alongside the established main organization**, which provides space for free thinkers. In this way both forms of organization can play to their strengths.

Every idea that is born at the blue level flows into a process. Disruptive ideas therefore often have a hard time. Idea generation works very well in blue companies with process-oriented idea generation workshops.

2.4 Orange: Financial incentives for ideas

On the orange level, ideas similar to red are created mainly when they contribute to one's own success. The difference from red, however, is that here it is also believed that existing systems must be taken into account in order to be successful. For example, one is aware that ideas in an organization must go through certain decision-making processes, but at the same time one tries to speed up these processes for one's own ideas; for example, by holding informal discussions with relevant decision-makers.

At orange, **financial incentives** are a good way to increase the amount of ideas, but **increasing the visibility** of the individual—for example, through an idea competition—can also increase the motivation to contribute ideas.

Developing ideas outside the norm is quite common when they have a positive impact on one's own success.

Examples

A **large trading company** *encourages its employees to submit new ideas on a regular basis. A business case is always to be calculated for each of the suggestions, showing what the implementation would cost and what profit the organization would gain from it within two years. As a side effect, this approach also intensively promotes entrepreneurial thinking. The innovators are rewarded with a percentage of the savings or profit.*

As part of a performance review meeting, a **logistics group** *has built a fixed category into each management dialogue, in which innovative suggestions are expected from each employee, depending on their task or function.*

The best suggestions are then adopted and implemented at the department meeting at the end of the year. Not bringing a proposal is not accepted.

Dangers

Ideas must always have a **clear chance of success** on the orange level in order to be accepted. Longer incubation and reflection phases, on the other hand, are rather difficult to implement. Since the quality of ideas often correlates with the amount of reflection time, there is a risk that the idea generation process will focus on **quick wins** and that "big" ideas will be perceived as too elaborate and unspecific and will be rejected accordingly.

Tips

The use of ideas for (personal) success is an important motivating factor in an orange company. Those who manage to combine status and recognition in the company with the development of new ideas will transform an orange culture into an idea machine. Even in longer innovation projects, **transparent and regular communication of success** is important to maintain the orange organization's support for the goal.

Ideas in orange companies are generated when they contribute to the individual's success as well as that of the company. At orange, financial incentives and status benefits are a good way to increase the amount of ideas. 30

2.5 Green: Finding ideas with a sense of unity

In green companies, people like to collaborate and forge ideas with one another—this also applies to people from different groups and different areas. This **high degree of heterogeneity** promotes innovation and new ideas. Ideas are discussed openly and in a very appreciative manner. The participants of innovation workshops are always on fire because the joint development of ideas appeals to the green community spirit. New ideas are first of all generally evaluated positively here. Mistakes are seen as part of a learning process. The enrichment of ideas also works very well with green, because **ideas** are **generally regarded as a community project**.

Examples

A very successful **IT consultancy** *uses the World Café method during its annual company meeting. Every employee, regardless of position, location, or departmental affiliation, is allowed to take part and develop innovations together with others on existing problems.*

As the name World Café describes, the topics are discussed here in informal and coffee-house-like settings, free of hierarchy and self-controlled. Ideas and thoughts are visualized on tablecloths with colored pens. In this way, the topic owner collects many thoughts from colleagues in a consensus-oriented dialogue.

Innovation rounds and open-space events are used by an electronics company to bring people together on a voluntary basis to discuss topics and issues. Moderators support this basically self-controlling process. The voluntariness and the openness of the topics guarantees a high level of participation and energy. No participant is "committed" or "sent." The principle applies: all people who come are the right ones, and all topics that come up are relevant.

Dangers

In the workshop setting, participants at the green level sometimes find it difficult to decide on an idea. **The process of brainstorming is often more important than the actual implementation.** Nevertheless, at some point during the brainstorming process, you come to a point where you have to say goodbye to the less good ideas. However, it is not easy for people at this stage because they do not want to treat anyone badly, which makes it even more difficult to make a decision.

In general, care must always be taken to ensure that ideas do not remain at their conceptual status here but are implemented later. However, this often requires a very high level of personal commitment, someone who is willing to fight with elbows for an idea—difficult in a green culture, especially since the implementation of disruptive ideas often sees losers in the system.

Tips

The green work culture is ideal for the development of new ideas that have a high level of acceptance among many different stakeholders. Those who further promote and support the high degree of heterogeneity and provide scope for the development of ideas have a solid basis for a steady stream of good ideas.

But also make sure that the implementation of ideas is in focus, so that in the long run no frustration arises due to ideas that have gotten stuck in the concept status.

30 *The enrichment of ideas works very well with green, because ideas are generally regarded as a joint project here. The high degree of heterogeneity resulting from the coming together of people from different groups and departments promotes innovation and thus new ideas. In general, green always has to make sure that ideas are implemented.*

2.6 Yellow: The innovation level par excellence

Many start-ups are developed by yellow founders for whom a green organization has become too narrow. The whole focus here is on solving a relevant problem; the inspiration comes from a "big idea." **Freedom and individuality** are also an important part of the culture, and **goals are more important than processes**. In innovation projects, making mistakes is allowed, as long as this results in a learning effect for the organization.

Yellow managers ask their employees specifically for ideas and let them participate in their implementation. They know that it is successful when heterogeneous teams work together and everyone can contribute ideas.

Yellow organizations know how to use the different skills of the all levels appropriately; they have recognized that **diversity is the key** to the success of an innovation culture. The development of the corporate culture is seen as an important success factor.

Examples

Google is extremely success oriented, but employee participation is an important part of the company culture. The ideas of the employees are not only in demand but are also promoted by many incentives. Lifelong learning and the further development of employees are also very important. However, this is not done for altruistic motives; rather, it is important to stay ahead in the tough competition for the best minds in Silicon Valley.

A **management consultancy** operates in a very yellow business model; that is, loosely networked, working together on demand, promoting coexistence. It uses the network to develop new ideas. For this purpose, new media are used in a situation-specific way to activate the virtual network. Thus, virtual platforms are used on a mobile basis to link traveling consultants to generate ideas. Everyone contributes but without claiming ownership of the result.

Dangers

If an organization started by yellow founders grows, the organizational structures often change and **blue-dominated processes** emerge. As a result, employees with a yellow background no longer feel comfortable and may leave the company or lose their energy.

Tips

Yellow organizations have many opportunities to provide **the optimal resources for a powerful innovation culture**:

- Innovation rooms or innovation labs provide the necessary change of focus for the development of ideas.
- Flexible working time models allow the necessary time freedom.
- Regular networking events with external experts provide the inspiration for new approaches.

In the **growth phase**, yellow organizations should pay special attention to the culture of innovation, because this is where structures often emerge that slow down and restrict the yellow flow of thought.

Yellow companies have many opportunities to create a culture of innovation in their organization if they are careful to provide the necessary resources. In growth phases, care should be taken not to lose the yellow entrepreneurial spirit. 30

2.7 Turquoise: Value-oriented idea development

In turquoise companies, trading is no longer exclusively controlled by profit maximization. Instead, the common good and global responsibility are an important part of the organization.
The term "**social innovation**" is often used in connection with entrepreneurs who think in turquoise. Their innovations focus on implementing projects that have a positive impact on the way people live together and the community. Spirituality and sustainability are an essential part of communication and also influence decision-making in innovation processes. This means that responsibility for social action is not left to the state but is seen as a basic corporate principle.
Some start-ups emerge from a turquoise idea but are often "overrun" by other levels during the implementation phase.

Examples

There are no exclusively turquoise companies. **Google**'s beginnings **with the motto "Don't be evil"** are an example of a turquoise starting point, but nowadays it has certainly been pushed back by yellow.

The outdoor manufacturer **Vaude** *has many turquoise traits in its corporate culture and policy. Antje von Dewitz, the daughter of the company founder, Albrecht von Dewitz, follows this path consistently and sustainably. In the company's anniversary publication* Gipfelbuch 1974–2014, *she formulates the claim that the company must be innovative, functional, and also environmentally friendly. The company is committed to responsible sourcing and production. Innovation here also arises from the turquoise claim of social responsibility, which is both local and global.*

Dangers

Often turquoise ideas **conflict with the compulsion to make money and be successful in the market**. Particularly in growth phases, there is a great danger that turquoise organizations will be overrun by other levels and thus lose their original mentality.

Tips

Turquoise organizations usually also have a good proportion of employees who are at other levels. Often it is a great challenge to pass on the turquoise view, which is very systemic and sustainable, to the organization. It is important to keep this in mind, as well as growth phases, because it is precisely in these phases that other levels can quickly gain the upper hand and change the character of the company.

The knowledge about the development stage of a company helps to establish innovation successfully. Innovation is relevant for the following seven levels of the 9 Levels of Value Systems: 30

- *Purple: For innovation to succeed here, the patriarch or matriarch must be involved.*
- *Red: Competition and rivalry promote the development of ideas here.*
- *Blue: At this level, process-oriented idea-finding workshops are useful.*
- *Orange: Incentives such as financial rewards motivate the development of ideas.*
- *Green: The joint development of ideas is successful, but sometimes there is a lack of implementation.*
- *Yellow: The yellow entrepreneurial spirit is ideal for producing innovations.*
- *Turquoise: Sustainability and systemic thinking play a major role in the generation of ideas.*

30 MINUTES

3. Dealing with resistance

If you want to establish a culture of innovation in your company, on the one hand you have to create the conditions for it, but on the other hand the question of how to **deal with resistance** is also important—because this can lead to the measures that have been started coming to nothing in the second step. Many people reject new things at first, especially if they bring about changes for themselves. The introduction of an innovation culture also means that employees have to leave their comfort zone. This may well lead to stubborn resistance. Now it is important to get the resistors on board and to get them enthusiastic about the Innovation Culture project. This chapter will show you how this works.

3.1 Resistance and its origin

Just as the levels of the 9 Levels of Value Systems are all different, so too their expression in individual people on one level is different. It can therefore by no means be taken for granted that all values of a value level are 100 percent appropriate for someone at this level of development. As a result, someone may **feel reluctant** and develop resistance to an innovation or measure **at their own value level**. This may not be expected at first, but it is precisely what creates conflicts, which are stirred up when the individual characteristics of a value level are not sufficiently taken into account in a particular person.

For the measures that are taken to establish a culture of innovation, this means that in addition to the classification in terms of the 9 Levels of Value Systems, it is also important to know the characteristics of the individual at a certain level—and thus the dislikes that this person feels. Only in this way can an **understanding of resistance** exist, which can then be used or reversed with the appropriate approach.

Resistance can be measured

Just as you can measure values and present the results in the form of the 9 Levels of Value Systems, it is also possible to measure resistance. In order to better explain how to measure resistance, we would first like to show you what is meant by a resistance in terms of the theory of the 9 Levels of Value Systems. Using the examples in section 3.3, we will once again illustrate what this means in practice.

Resistance in general

A resistance is a will, an action, a force, or a movement that is perceived as a counteraction to another movement or measure. From a management perspective, a resistance is a **negative reaction to changes** that take place; for example, in structures, processes, or entire systems.

Resistance occurs above all when proven structures or process flows are changed or abolished by individual employees. Affected employees experience changes—even those that could represent an improvement for them—first of all as a disturbance. They regard the change as unwelcome, as something that restricts their freedom, and want the old state to be restored.

Whether resistance is expressed rather weakly or very intensively depends, among other things, on how serious the restriction is from the point of view of the person affected and how intensively he or she is prepared to offer resistance.

Resistance can also be regarded as a **protective function**. This is the case when people, teams, or organizations try to protect themselves from the supposedly nonsensical or harmful change. However, resistance **in the context of a change process** can **also be desirable**, because this is how those involved signal interest and concern. Resistance also brings information to the table that helps managers to get to know the needs of their employees. One of the main tasks in the change process is to **incorporate resistance into the change process by means of suitable measures**. This approach can be used to channel resistance in people, departments, or the company as a whole into productive paths. It is also possible to use appropriate techniques for conflict resolution. If someone has resistance to value systems or value levels, this is shown by the fact that the person does not agree with the values and the thought and behavior patterns derived from them. Exactly the opposite occurs: there is a counterreaction. Depending on one's own value level, this can take on different dimensions and intensities.

Resistance in innovation processes

Resistance can basically be understood as defensive attitudes or aversions to specific value levels. In innovation processes, it can therefore happen that a method or a process causes resistance in a person, a group, or even entire organizations because the associated value level does not correspond to one's own. This makes it all the more important that innovation methods and processes fit the general value culture of the company—otherwise it won't work. Nevertheless, due to the individual differences already described, resistance is always to be expected and must be countered appropriately.

30

On each value level are specific characteristics. This leads to the possibility that someone could also develop resistance to changes that correspond to his or her own value level. One should be aware of this. This is the only way to understand resistance, which can then be used or reversed with the appropriate approach.

3.2 Resistance to value systems

Of course, each level can also cause resistance. The reasons for this can be completely different. It is possible, for example, that the person concerned has a low degree of a level and is therefore simply unfamiliar with the value systems that characterize it. But it is also possible that he or she has had **negative experiences** with this value system, which are the trigger for the resistance. Another possible reason is, for example, that the value systems the person is confronted with are **contrary to his or her own value systems**. Here are two examples.

- *If a person has the main characteristic green and prefers cooperative and consensus-oriented agreements, a red value system, which prefers quick and situational decisions—in case of doubt, without agreement – can cause resistance.*
- *If the main characteristic is purple and rituals and traditions are adhered to, this often creates resistance*

with orange, because people with a purple attitude are progress or growth inhibitors from the perspective of the orange level.

If people, groups, or organizations know their own value systems, they also know at the same time what level they reject and/or resist. **Measuring this resistance is so important because this is where the problems in everyday life arise.** People do not feel well, tensions arise in groups, and conflicts surface in organizations—the reason is in all cases that value systems cause resistance.

Four possible combinations

There are exactly four possibilities in the interaction of value systems and the resistance directed against them:

1. Low level and low resistance

If this combination exists, the **value system** is **not strongly developed**. At the same time, there is **little resistance to it.**

If you take the example of a blue level, this could mean that the blue is not very pronounced but also that the person does not have any problems with this value system. Maybe the person is just happy if everything is well organized.

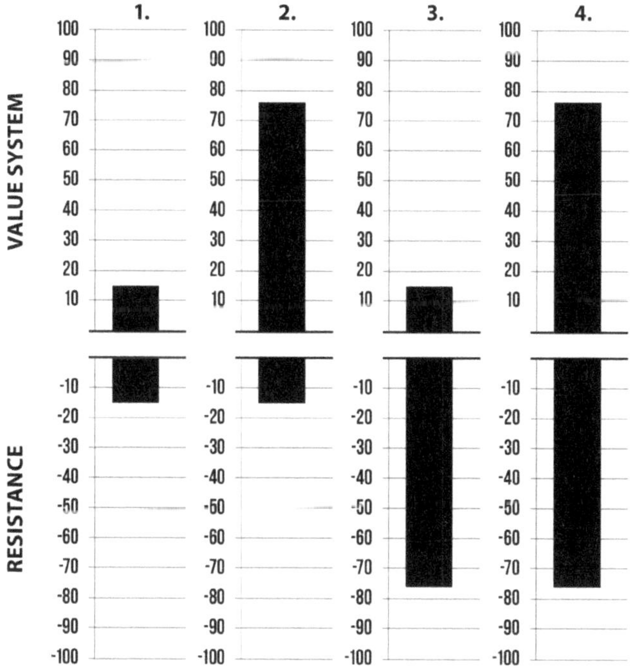

Fig. 1: Four possible combinations of value systems and resistance

2. High character of the level and low resistance

In this combination, the **values of this level** are **strongly pronounced** and thus guide action. At the same time there is **hardly any resistance to this level**

An example of this is purple: purple people have strong ties to their homeland, love rituals, and bond over long periods of time. It practically goes without saying that people with similar value systems are very happy to be accepted into the community and that there will be no resistance against them.

3. Low level and high resistance

In such a combination, the value system is **not very pronounced** on the one hand, but at the same time **the value system disturbs the person**.

Taking orange as an example, this could mean that the dynamics, goal orientation, proactivity, and so on of orange are not very pronounced in a person. At the same time, these very values disturb this person when he or she comes into contact with them.

4. High character of the level and high resistance

If this combination is present, one also speaks of **ambivalence**. In this case, a system of values is **very strong**, but at the same time it causes **rejection**.

An example of this is people with strong red values: such people prefer values like dominance, strength, power, and assertiveness. At the same time, however, they feel resistance when another person approaches them with the same values and is even more dominant and powerful than they are.

Not only can people be assigned to a certain value level, but they can also develop resistance to a value level. If people, groups, or organizations know their own value systems, they also know the level against which they feel resistance. Measuring this resistance is so important because this is where the problems in everyday life arise. 30

3.3 Examples from everyday life

Why does someone have problems with a situation or another person? Why does one person aim to maximize profit while the other person is completely apathetic? Why is it that someone can't cope with corporate structures but is completely at home in loose networking activities? Everyday life is full of colors—the colors of the 9 levels. The following examples illustrate what makes the person described "tick." With this knowledge people gain a **better understanding of themselves** and their behavior or decisions. In addition, such an analysis **facilitates cooperation** considerably.

The head of department (green)

A department head of a rather green-run company has a very cooperative and consensus-oriented management attitude. He has massive problems if the red value system appears in his department or if he is confronted with it from outside the department. This even causes him health problems. His strong green preference and the low proportion of red values make it difficult for him to stand up to red.

He also feels a high level of resistance to purple, which he interprets as follows: "It bothers me when employees cling to traditional procedures or when employees feel protected just because their father is a divisional manager."

The creative, freethinking coach (yellow)

This coach works as a sparring partner, is very free spirited, and is reluctant to act in administrative and excessively business-oriented projects. If she comes into contact with projects that require a lot of bureaucracy and structured administrative work—that is, projects that are assigned to the blue level—she can carry them out, but only with reluctance. If a project is too focused on processes or solely on maximizing profits, she finds this disturbing.

The former expat (turquoise)

For this IT expert and head of department who is returning after five years of working abroad, it is hard to imagine returning to the German headquarters. He feels trapped in the rather rigid blue constructs, some of which are corruptly (red) infiltrated.

There can be various reasons for resistance to change and innovation; for example,

- ***People encounter a value system that is foreign to them.***
- ***People are confronted with values that are contrary to their own.***
- ***Even within a value system there are different individual characteristics that can lead to resistance.***

An analysis of individuals' value systems increases their understanding of themselves and facilitates cooperation.

30 MINUTES

4. Innovation culture in practice

The theory is one thing; to put it into practice is quite another. Leadership plays a decisive role here, because it not only sets an example but is the key to whether and how the topic of innovation is approached in the company. It is up to managers to use the appropriate innovation tools and to create an innovation-promoting atmosphere in the team. They must be aware that it can be fatal to simply let themselves be driven by so-called patent remedies. These may have worked wonderfully for another company but are not suitable for their own cultural environment. So what must leadership do specifically to bring innovation into the company? What does it take to establish a culture of innovation?

4.1 Appropriate innovation methods

A basic prerequisite for successful innovation is that the management is aware of the different levels at which they themselves, the organization, and its employees find themselves—but also of the different tools at their disposal. After all, establishing a powerful innovation culture always means using the right creativity techniques. The choice of the right tools can also be made on the basis of value levels. There are methods that are particularly well suited to individual value levels, as well as those that should not be used at certain levels.

We would like to present a few examples without explaining the method in detail, as this would go beyond the scope of this book. The aim is rather to give you an overview of the various tools and to develop an understanding of which innovation method might be suitable for practical application in your company.

Brainstorming—Works for all who follow the "golden rule"

Brainstorming is certainly the classic among creativity techniques. One of the "golden rules" of brainstorming is do not criticize! Because **quantity leads to quality**. In practice, however, this rule is often broken. For example, difficulties can arise if blue, purple, or red value systems predominate:

- With **blue groups**, it can quickly happen that new ideas are devalued because they do not fit into the familiar set of rules. The danger is particularly great in brainstorming, because here the ideas are often already rejected in the development phase and are not given the chance to develop further.
- When working with **purple** and **red groups**, care must be taken to ensure that the boss does not lead and dominate the action too much. Nonverbal communication can also be used to show rejection.

Tip: Brainwriting—a brainstorming variant in which spontaneous ideas are first written down—can be helpful if participants find it difficult to express their opinions to others or their supervisor.

Visioning work and dream journeys—Ideal for green and yellow

In this creative method, participants let their guards down and give their thoughts a space to freely dream up the vision of the organization. This method is very effective, but it works only if the participants can get involved—and if a moderator strings together pictures, experiences, and stories "level by level" in this process.

Such imaginative methods are rather unsuitable for **red** or **blue organizations**, as they seem too esoteric or are even dismissed as "granola." Green and yellow groups, on the other hand, are very happy to get involved. **Orange groups** need to be guided purposefully through the innovation process to achieve good results.

Innovation digging—Blue will love it

The method of "innovation digging" is a wonderfully structured and, in a figurative sense, **"hard working" method**. This alone is a reason why it is especially suitable for **blue-digging** groups and brings out great ideas. There are clear procedures and fields to be worked on. In this way it is possible to generate a lot of creative approaches within a tight structure. This is exactly what inspires blue groups.
Orange on the other hand feels slowed down by too much structure. This technique is also rather unsuitable for **green groups**, as they do not find room for discussion.

30 *The choice of innovation methods to be used in brainstorming should also consider the value levels of the participants. For example, blue groups appreciate structured techniques, while green and yellow are open to visioning work and dream journeys.*

4.2 The role of leadership

It turns out to be not so easy to establish ideas and the resulting innovations in a company. This is all the more true if it also means a change for the individual. The consequence: resistance increases. Now it is up to the management to establish a culture of innovation that is open to ideas. **The leader becomes the innovation leader.** First of all, there is the question of where the process should be located: Doesn't innovation belong in the research and development department or even in marketing? In fact, the greatest potential lies in **process or organizational development**. This is because this area is closely linked to how employees work together and how they communicate—among themselves and with other departments. Ideas that emerge here can have a large impact on the whole organization.

The manager's task
The manager has the task of empowering the company and with it the employees to react flexibly to the changes and challenges of the constantly changing world and at the same time to develop themselves further.

Especially in **medium-sized companies** we observe how ideas come almost exclusively from the management level and are then passed on to the employees with the expectation that the ideas will be implemented exactly. This classic approach is extremely dangerous. If something changes at the management level, the ideas are lost at the same time. The consequences are obvious.

Not all employees are the same

Some employees welcome the fact that they can work according to clearly defined guidelines. **Generation Y** in particular, however, expects a different kind of cooperation with the management: these young employees want to understand what advantages an idea might have, and they also want to play an active **role in the brainstorming process** themselves.

Management should only moderate innovation processes instead of providing ideas top down.

How you drive innovation

What concrete steps can you now take as a manager if you want to promote innovation in your company?

Find and promote innovation drivers

Innovation drivers are the people you need to drive innovation forward in your company and to establish a culture of innovation. This does not refer to those who are constantly coming up with new ideas but to people who, through their curiosity, openness, and enthusiasm for new things, **help others to follow suit**. They view every new project optimistically and are always looking for ways to bring the project to a successful conclusion. Until the next project is due.

Create innovation spaces

When do you have the best ideas? Certainly not when you are asked to develop a solution at your desk within the next two hours. Ideas are rarely born in the normal course of day-to-day business but rather come like a **flash of inspiration** in the shower, while mowing the lawn, or when jogging in the forest. It has even been scientifically proven that the human brain starts to make new connections from nerve cell to nerve cell when the daily rush slowly disappears.

So create innovation spaces where your employees can **retreat** and **switch to a different work mode**.

Be happy about new problems

Whoever avoids problems acts as a brake on ideas. The explanation is simple: **an idea is created on the basis of a problem**. Or formulated the other way around: there is no idea that is not based on a problem.

So if you want to establish an innovation culture in your company, you have to **welcome problems**. If a problem arises, you should approach it as simply as possible. Question why something is the way it is right now and whether it could be completely different, and examine all eventualities very intensively. You will be amazed at the results.

Search for structured ideas

There are processes for everything in your company—why not also for brainstorming?

Please do not confuse this tip with the well-known company suggestion system. Radical innovations in particular often get lost in such a system.

Structured searches for ideas can be carried out using various methods, such as the **innovation digging** mentioned in the previous chapter. Here, creative forces are bundled to regularly develop new ideas. Comparable to the world of professional treasure hunting, this method—like a treasure map—proceeds in a search field matrix in which search areas are entered. The **probability of finding great ideas and innovations increases** significantly with the help of this technique. Just imagine how much more motivated you will be to create ideas when you realize that most ideas have long been in the heads of your employees!

Ask the right questions
The following reflection questions will help you to promote innovation in your company:

- Who in your company could be an innovation driver?
- In which context do the best ideas arise in your company?
- How could you focus on potential problems?
- In which way would it be possible for you to set up a system for structured idea generation?

Eyes open for the team selection

Finally, a few words about the composition of a suitable team: of course, it is pleasant to have a well-functioning team in which **everyone is on the same wavelength**, if only for the reason that the potential for conflict is considerably reduced. However, a team constellation of this kind often does not deliver the best ideas. The reason is that the tried and tested and familiar are not readily given up and replaced by the new and thus unknown. On the other hand, the more diverse the team, the greater the chance of finding truly innovative solutions. The greater the **diversity**, the more different the specialist skills and the points of view. For a manager this means a special challenge. It is in the hands of the management to guide a team with a high level of diversity to deal with these differences openly. In this way, conflicts are addressed instead of being sat out. The result is **significantly higher productivity and creativity** than with teams that harmonize from the ground up.

Managers have the task of enabling employees to develop and change. The differences between employees must also be taken into account: for example, it is important for Generation Y to be involved in brainstorming. 30

4.3 What can go wrong

Mistakes are made. But you can learn a lot from these mistakes. What worked wonderfully for another company and astounded everyone may be a total failure for you. Here we have given you a few examples from our work that show you how with the wrong approach the

plan to establish a culture of innovation can really go wrong. This is especially true if the existing value level of the organization is not taken into account.
You will understand why we do not mention any names or company names here. It could even be your company . . .

The blue company that wants to become Google

After a visit to Silicon Valley, the management of a medium-sized company with a strong hierarchical structure is enthusiastic about this "different working atmosphere." They were particularly taken with the work rooms, with their **open architecture** and **playful furnishings**, which were more reminiscent of children's rooms.
After the management returns home, the first project is immediately underway: the creation of a special innovation room, with many of the same furnishings as those seen in California. Even a swing will be installed.
After completion, however, they are surprised that no employee uses this space for the development of ideas. Instead, employees meet in the room only for a cup of cappuccino during the coffee break.
This is mainly due to the fact that the prevailing corporate culture has **no use for the purpose of the room**. People are used to working within the traditional work organization. To take the liberty of sitting in the swing for a few hours is unthinkable.

The purple company that blocks ideas

A smaller medium-sized mechanical engineering company has a successful history behind it. Patents that were developed some time ago are the basis for a very good market position. Essentially, these developments were initiated by the company founder and managing director, who still spends a large part of his time in research and development. In order to further advance the company, the company boss has hired a young up-and-coming engineer, who starts right away and brings a whole range of new project ideas to meetings. But time and again the CEO stops him with words like, "That's nice, but it won't work," or **"We've never done it like this before."** The junior engineer looks at this for three months and then quits to move to another company. The company loses an important employee.

The green company whose discussions make decisions difficult

There is a good team culture in the HR department of a company. People enjoy working together, new projects are discussed together, and everyone can contribute their thoughts in meetings. Employees' ideas are also regularly collected and discussed.

It becomes difficult when it has to be decided which ideas are to be implemented. Here the team has a hard time, **ideas are discussed to death**, and they are at best implemented only in a weakened form. Only when a decision process with methods for strategic idea evaluation is used does the situation improve.

The red company that creates idea silos

The sales department of an insurance company works very successfully, the insurance agents have great individual freedom, and each is responsible for a delimited area.

The new sales manager decides to visit all sales offices and get to know his employees. He quickly notices that despite the group's process guidelines, work processes differ greatly in the individual areas. For example, while digitization is making little headway in the group as a whole, two years ago one sales office developed an app on its own initiative that allows customer meetings to be conducted much more successfully.

As there is no regular platform for the exchange of information in the sales team, this idea did not become known, nor was the distributor himself **interested in sharing his idea on his own initiative**.

The orange company that stays on the ground

A medium-sized trading company maintains a proactive approach to innovation. New ideas are not only collected but explicitly requested. The submission of new suggestions is even part of the employee assessment.

In the case of the ideas submitted, particular attention is paid to the speed of implementation. Ideas that can be implemented very quickly, so-called **quick wins**, are preferred and positively evaluated. Ideas are often implemented in exactly the same way as they are submitted; there are no supplementary rounds to enrich the ideas. As a result, **small-scale solutions** remain, and the urgently needed transformation of the business model is not pursued, as this means a longer innovation process.

It is up to managers alone to use the appropriate innovation tools and to create an innovation-promoting atmosphere in the team. This makes them innovation leaders.
The greatest potential for innovation lies in process and organizational development. It is closely linked to how employees work together and how they communicate—with each other and with other departments.
The tasks of leadership are as follows:

- *finding and promoting innovation drivers*
- *creating innovation spaces*
- *welcoming problems*
- *searching for ideas in a structured way*
- *paying attention to diversity in team building*

It is always important to make sure that techniques and measures also fit the value system and culture of the company. Only then can they be successful and lead to innovative ideas and their implementation.

Innovation and the 9 levels

The model of the 9 Levels of Value Systems gives an overview of the different value systems of individuals, groups, or organizations. Seven of the 9 levels are relevant with regard to innovation.
The following is a summary of the prevailing attitude toward innovation at these levels and what needs to be considered.

Level purple

The owner has innovation sovereignty.

- Disruptive innovations have a rather tough time with purple.
- If the owner is involved at an early stage, innovative ideas can prevail.
- This is best achieved with the help of a neutral third party as moderator.

Level red

Ideas emerge driven by success.

- Red organizations love competition.
- Innovations are best created in direct competition.
- Immediate reward systems work wonders.

Level blue

Ideas flow through systems.

- Organizations on the blue level are strong in incremental innovation.

- Process-oriented idea-finding workshops work well.
- These workshops should bring together people from different hierarchical and organizational levels.

Level orange

Financial incentives push the idea generation process.

- If you combine the development of new ideas with status and recognition, this culture becomes an idea machine.
- The communication of success is very important—especially in longer projects.
- Ideas must always have clear prospects of success.

Level green

The strong sense of unity gives you wings.

- The promotion of heterogeneity and a freedom in the development of ideas ensure a constant stream of good ideas.
- The implementation of the ideas must always be kept in mind.
- Moderators help with the implementation of the process.

Level yellow

This is the ideal level for innovation.

- Innovation rooms or innovation labs provide the necessary change of focus.
- Flexible working time models allow the necessary time freedom.

- Networking events with external experts provide inspiration for new approaches.

Level turquoise

Value orientation guides innovation.

- The focus is always on making the world a bit better.
- Organizations on the turquoise level must not be overrun by other levels—especially during growth phases.
- People at this level create added value for the world by looking at the whole.

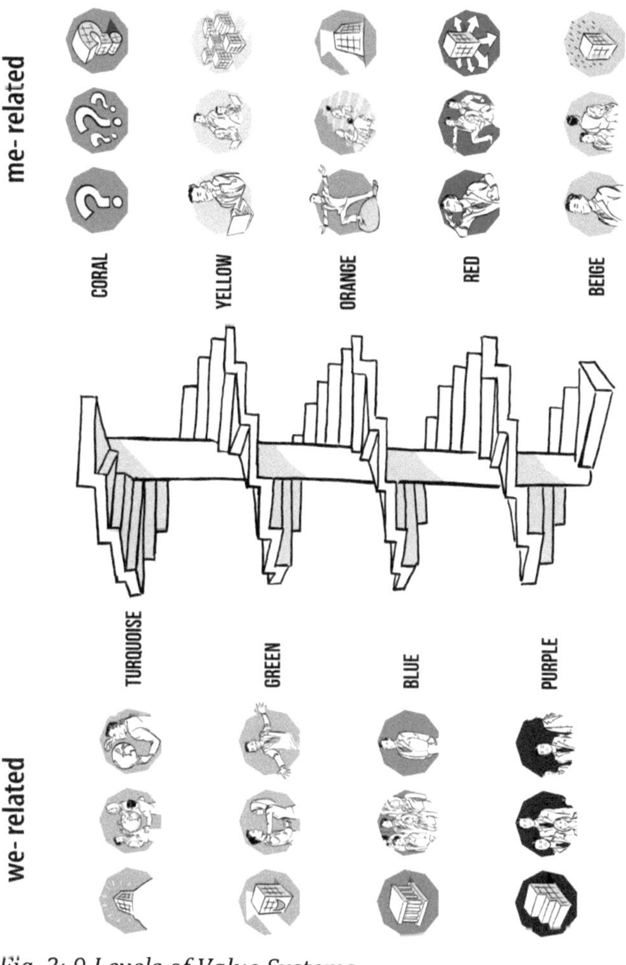

Fig. 2: 9 Levels of Value Systems

Fast reader

1. Innovation culture

"How do I manage to be innovative with my company?" This is a question that companies of all sizes are asking themselves. The reason? Today, only those who stand out from the crowd with a service or a product will be able to survive on the market in the long term.
But often initiatives such as research and development activities, the introduction of innovation departments, or even their own incubators for start-ups do not bring the desired output. Many therefore look for a patent remedy, but this is the wrong way to go. The solution lies in the individuality of each company and the people in it. You need knowledge about the value systems of people, teams, and organizations to find the right approach to establishing a culture of innovation for your own company.

Only those who not only develop their business model and product portfolio but radically change it will be successful in the long term. This requires certain prerequisites:

- ***empowered employees***
- ***flat hierarchies that leave room for creativity***
- ***supportive executives***
- ***resources for creative projects***
- ***diverse teams***
- ***incentive systems that support innovation***
- ***communication structures that offer open spaces***

2. The stages of the innovation culture

Each person is at his or her own personal stage of development, from which the topic of innovation is approached very individually. The model of the 9 Levels of Value Systems, which is based on the research work of Clare W. Graves and was further developed into an analysis tool by Rainer Krumm, offers orientation in this context. Just like individuals, organizations can also be assigned to a certain level of development, which significantly shapes their culture and thus also their approach to the topic of innovation. Without this knowledge of the differences in dealing with innovation, a planned innovation project can be doomed to failure from the outset.

30 ***On seven of the nine development levels, which are marked by colors in the system of the 9 levels, the topic of innovation can play a role:***

- ***Purple: The involvement of the patriarch or matriarch is important.***
- ***Red: Competition promotes the development of ideas.***
- ***Blue: Idea generation should be systematic and structured.***
- ***Orange: Innovation can be encouraged through incentives.***
- ***Green: Ideas are developed in a team.***
- ***Yellow: This is the innovation level par excellence.***
- ***Turquoise: Innovation is also value oriented here.***

3. Dealing with resistance

Even between people who are on the same value level, there are individual differences, which are expressed for example in dislikes or resistance. In addition to the assignment in terms of the 9 levels, it is therefore also important to know the individual characteristics of each level. This is the only way to understand resistance, which can then be used or reversed with the appropriate approach.

In innovation processes, it is possible that an innovation method or a process causes resistance in a person, a group, or even entire organizations. This makes it all the more important that innovation methods and processes fit the value culture of people and organizations—otherwise it will not work.

For the following reasons it is important in an innovation process to measure resistance: 30

- ***It becomes clear who cannot work with whom and why.***
- ***Mutual understanding is created, which facilitates agreements.***
- ***Behaviors and decisions become comprehensible.***
- ***Slowdowns in progress and growth become visible.***

4. Innovation culture in practice

A basic prerequisite for successful innovation is that the management is aware of the different tools—but also of the different levels at which they, the organization, and its employees are loca-

ted. The manager has the task of empowering the company and with it the employees to react flexibly to the changes and challenges of the constantly changing world and at the same time to develop themselves further.

30 ***The tasks of leadership in finding innovations are as follows:***

- ***Find and promote innovation drivers among employees.***
- ***Create spaces that support innovation.***
- ***Welcome problems, because they are the best source of ideas.***
- ***Structure the idea generation process.***
- ***Put together "colorful" teams.***
- ***Consider the context in which the best ideas are generated.***
- ***Look for a way to systematically set up idea generation.***
- ***Manage in a value-oriented manner.***

The authors

Rainer Krumm is a management trainer, consultant, and coach. He studied business education and strategic management and has advised, trained, and coached international companies, top executives, and teams in over 20 countries. He is considered one of the most experienced international consultants and trainers in the field of corporate culture and change management—based on the developmental psychology of Prof. Clare W. Graves.
He is both founder and managing owner of axiocon GmbH, a management consultancy specializing in organizational and value management, and of the 9 Levels Institute for Value Systems GmbH & Co KG—an institute that develops and distributes the scientifically proven analysis tools for the 9 levels model, which have been tested in practice. The Ravensburg-based institute specializes in the development and distribution of analysis tools for value systems.
www.9levels.com www.axiocon.de

Christian Buchholz is an expert in leadership and innovation. For more than 15 years, he has been sharing his knowledge and inspiration on the topic of "thinking differently" in lectures, seminars, and workshops. He has accompanied a large number of companies in different industries and countries during change processes and supported them in creating a sustainable culture of innovation.
He is cofounder and shareholder of the Verrocchio Institute for Innovation Competence, which bundles and disseminates innovation know-how. In this role he supports customers with an international team in the development of an efficient innovation and corporate culture.
www.christianbuchholz.com
www.verrocchio-institute.com

Related literature

- Krumm, R.: 9 Levels of Value Systems, werdewelt Verlag, Bicken, 3. erweiterte Auflage, 2017
- Buchholz, C.: Führungsmethoden für eine leistungsstarke Innovationskultur, aus: Die besten Ideen für erfolgreiche Führung, GABAL Verlag, Offenbach, 1. Auflage, 2014
- Buchholz, C., van Aerssen B The Innovator's Dictionary, De Gruyter, Berlin, 1. Auflage, 2020
- Krumm, R.: 30 Minuten für werteorientiertes Führen, GABAL Verlag, Offenbach, 2. Auflage, 2014
- Bär, M., Krumm, R., Wiehle, H.: Unternehmen verstehen, gestalten, verändern – Das Graves Value System in der Praxis, Gabler Verlag, Wiesbaden, 3. erweiterte Auflage, 2014
- Meyer, J.-U.: Erfolgsfaktor Innovationskultur – Das Innovationsmanagement der Zukunft, BusinessVillage, Göttingen, 2011
- Graves, C. W., Madden, H. T.: The Congruent Management Strategy, o. O., 1970

- Brandt-Biesler, F., Krumm, R.: So wird verkauft! Werteorientiertes Verkaufen mit den 9 Levels, GABAL Verlag, Offenbach, 2014
- Kienbaum.com: Deutsche Fachkräfte wollen flache Hierarchien und klare Ansagen, Pressemitteilung vom 22.03.2017
- capgemini.com: Studie: Unternehmenskulturelle Aspekte behindern die digitale Transformation, Pressemitteilung vom 08.06.2017

Index